Wales
Edited by Donna Samworth

First published in Great Britain in 2008 by:
Young Writers
Remus House
Coltsfoot Drive
Peterborough
PE2 9JX
Telephone: 01733 890066
Website: www.youngwriters.co.uk

All Rights Reserved

© *Copyright Contributors 2008*

SB ISBN 978-1 84431 713 4

Foreword

Young Writers' Big Green Poetry Machine is a showcase for our nation's most brilliant young poets to share their thoughts, hopes and fears for the planet they call home.

Young Writers was established in 1991 to nurture creativity in our children and young adults, to give them an interest in poetry and an outlet to express themselves. Seeing their work in print will encourage them to keep writing as they grow, and become our poets of tomorrow.

Selecting the poems has been challenging and immensely rewarding. The effort and imagination invested by these young writers makes their poems a pleasure to enjoy reading time and time again.

Contents

Blaengwawr Primary School, Aberdare
Megan Lane (10)	1
Keila Muriel Bebb (10)	2
Megan Jones (10)	3
Amelia Mclean (10)	4
Thomas Downes (11)	5

Coedylan Primary School, Graigwen
Siân Alison Smith (8)	6
Megan Oliver (9)	7
James Hughes (8)	8
James Ramsay (11)	9
Tazkia Choudhury (8)	10
Megan Davies (9)	11
Leah Hallett (9)	12
Lucy Thomas (8)	13
Rachel Birch (8)	14
Mali Griffiths (8)	15
Kyle Rhys Adams (11), Lewis Jones & Flynn Randell (10)	16
Joel Christian (8)	17
Jessica Howells Mullen (7)	18
Elis Morgan Pryse (7)	19
Chloe Davies (11) & Chloe Willetts (10)	20
Lucas Hickman (10) & Joshua Powell (9)	21
Daniella Bedgood & Shannon Golubovic (9)	22
Rory McGlennon (11)	23
Ben Gooding (9)	24
Maddy Goodson (8)	25
Jasmine Lavery & Amy Davies (10)	26
Ethan Randell & Matthew Easton (10)	27
Ella Bartlett-Jones & Martha Okon (10)	28
Jesse White (10) & Mason Ian Pritchard (9)	29
Atalya Paige Edwards (7)	30
Mark James (10) & Rhys Shortman (11)	31
Rhys Grainger & Ryan Alex Wheeler (10)	32
Jocelyn Kress Churchill (9)	33
Joseph Kerslake (8)	34

Cwmbach Junior School, Aberdare
Elizabeth Wigmore (10) 35
Jai Mehta (9) 36
Owen Williams (9) 37
Eve Jones (9) 38
Bethan Hancock (9) 39
Lucy Ffion Thomas (9) 40
Callum Lucas (10) 41
Bethan Davies (10) 42
Cody Bansal (8) 43
Rhys Phillips (11) 44
Stefan Jones (10) 45
Mitchell Griffiths (10) 46
Jöe Davies (10) 47
Sasiwimon Davies (10) 48
Meirion Gratland (9) 49
Rachel Kathrens (9) 50
Jake Falcon (11) 51
Owain Evans (10) 52
Callum Quinn & Thomas (11) 53
Rhobet Bull & Kristian Enoch (11) 54
Georgia Louise Davies (11) 55
Kiera James (10) 56
Cory Thomas (11) 57
Jack Harris (11) 58
Deiniol Llewellyn (10) 59
Zoe Jayne Jones (10) 60
Sean Williams (11) 61
James Williams (11) 62
Abbie Kate Jones & Emily Watts (11) 63
Connor Llewellyn (11) 64

Gurnos CP School, Swansea
Nia Davie (10) 65
James Moore (11) 66
Abbie Lodwick (10) 67

Maindee Primary School, Newport
Tamzin Davies (8) 68
Mahida Rahman (8) 69
Callum Shaw (9) 70

Suhayb Tariq (9) 71
Rita Mwanza (9) 72

Pembroke Dock Community School, Pembroke Dock
Eleanor Baker (10) 73
Holly Adams (11) 74
Marcus Blair (11) 75
Amy Goodman (11) 76
Lucy Hearn (11) 77
Jake Evans (11) 78
Chloe Cardy (11) 79
Rhys James (10) 80
Ryan Edwards (11) 81
Emily Pyle 82
Ffion Howells (9) 83
Ben Lascelles (9) 84
Craig Jones (9) 85
Daniel Hearn (8) 86
Shauna Brereton (9) 87
Shannon Howells (9) 88
Derek Brundrett (8) 89
Ryan Bourner (9) 90
MJ Morgan (10) 91
Luke Hawkins (10) 92
Elle Davenport (11) 93
James Richard Beynon (11) 94
Ben Veal (10) 95
Ashton Scott (11) 96
Liam Gammer (11) 97
George Hancock (11) 98
Alicia Kingdom (10) 99
Jack Jamie Dow (11) 100
Tawny Davies (12) 101
Kayley Davies (11) 102
Jordan Wright (11) 103
Matthew Veal (11) 104
Leigh Jenkins (10) 105
Katherine Brookes (11) 106
Billy Kilpatrick (10) 107

Pengelli Primary School, Swansea
Eden Statham (8) — 108
Josh Hier (9) — 109
Francesca Anne Oak (9) — 110
Cameron Davey (8) — 111
Rhiannon Bevan (8) — 112
Ben Thomas (7) — 113
Courtney Lauren Huxtable (9) — 114
Chloë O'Hare (9) — 115
Cerys-Jade Hickman (8) — 116
David Ashley Symonds (7) — 117
Joe Davies (8) — 118
Liam Oak (11) — 119
Chloe Harding (10) — 120
Sara Piper (8) — 121
Ciaran Foley (9) — 122
Callum Davies (8) — 123
Millie Baker (10) — 124
Aneurin Donald (11) — 125
Nicole Clark — 126
Daisy South — 127

Rhayader Primary School, Rhayader
Jade Harriet Evans-Hope (9) — 128
Hana Albiston (8) — 129
Rupert Storer (9) — 130
Courtney Price (9) — 131
Breanna Joy Downey (9) — 132
Jacob Sylvester (9) — 133
Toby Lewis (9) — 134
Rebecca Findley (8) — 135
Nicole Williams (9) — 136

St Mary's Junior School, Caldicot
Reece Ware (11) — 137
Melissa Blenkiron (11) — 138
Chloe Bryant (11) — 139
Joseph Russ (11) — 140
Daniel Gates (11) — 141
Nia Leonard (11) — 142
Katy Hunt (11) — 143

Thomas James Hulme (10)	144
Meaghan Rowe (7)	145
Chloe Woodman (8)	146
Abigail Green (8)	147
Kelly Hooper (8)	148

St Mellons CW Primary School, Llanrumney

Shanice Taaffe (8)	149
Joanne Hares (9)	150
Chloe Thomas (8)	151
Hannah Graves (8)	152
Jack Voyle (8)	153
Jake Morgan (9)	154
William Adams (9)	155
Ieuan Burridge-Bryant (8)	156
Alicia Feneck (9)	157
Bryony Thomas (8)	158

St Monica's CW Primary School, Heath

Joshua McConnell (10)	159
Jamil Alam (9)	160
Lily Richards (10)	161
Patrick Jolly (9)	162
Kesia Osborne (10)	163

Trelewis Primary School, Merthyr Tydfil

Benjamin Caffell (8)	164
Thomas Matthews (8)	165
Sam Davies (9)	166
Amy Jones (8)	167
Callum Mayers (9)	168
Caragh Bell-Langford & Kira Thomas (9)	169
Christopher Jones (8) & Morgan Gwilym (9)	170

Ysgol Bryn Deva, Connah's Quay

Callum Crossley (8)	171
Emily Monteith-Roberts (10)	172
Shannon Baines (9)	173
Letitia Lovelock (10)	174
Daniel Wilson (9)	175

Kyle Villiers (10) 176
William Williamson (8) 177
Kelly Louise Walker (10) 178
Alessia Powell (10) 179
Ashleigh Claire Jones (10) 180
Philip Goff (10) 181
Deryn Phillips (11) 182
Amy Jane Gould (9) 183
Aimee Shaw (10) 184

Ysgol Owen Jones, Northop
Tom Blackwell 185
Corey Hunt (10) 186
Lucie Cansdale 187
Chloe Tivendale (11) 188
Cameron Williams (11) 189
Shivani Patel (11) 190
Katie Gemmell (11) 191
Nicole Askey (11) 192
Jack Hewitt (10) 193
Olivia Farrell 194
Conal Ghee 195
Tanya Van Ruth 196

The Poems

Ban The Bags

Birds flying in the air
Have no idea why bags are there
Deciding to look in the bags
Get their heads stuck and start to gag
They start to choke, it is no joke
Birds are dying when they should be flying
Through the clean, flowing air
It's a terrible thing for them to bear
This needs to stop, we need to take action
Do it now for our animals' satisfaction
There must be a solution for this pollution.

Megan Lane (10)
Blaengwawr Primary School, Aberdare

Plastic Bags

Plastic bags are ruining the world
They're killing animals such as birds
Birds were flying, but now they're dying
Stop pollution, there's always a solution
You never know what you might see
Harmful plastic is around some trees
Just get a 'bag for life'
And stop this trouble and strife.

Keila Muriel Bebb (10)
Blaengwawr Primary School, Aberdare

Pollution

Make the environment clean
Stop plastic bags ruining our streams
Birds were flying
Now they're dying
I'm not joking
Animals are choking
The sealife is dying
I'm not lying
Stop this pollution
And let's make a revolution.

Megan Jones (10)
Blaengwawr Primary School, Aberdare

Pollution

Stop pollution!
We need to make a resolution
Birds are dying while plastic bags are flying
Exotic creatures dying every minute

Let's stop this monstrosity and try to bin it
It's not fair on the animals
We are acting like criminals

Please buy a 'bag for life'
And the plastic bags will be knifed
So please stop pollution
Let's make a revolution.

Amelia Mclean (10)
Blaengwawr Primary School, Aberdare

Banish The Bags

Banish the bags, they're really bad
They're making us so mad
They're polluting the seas
And it's spreading disease
It's killing the life in the wild
The water's going mild
We need to stop it now, it's destroying our land
It's even on the sand
It's contagious, it's outrageous
It's a disgrace
It's gathering pace
The birds can't fly
As high in the sky
And they can't soar way up high
Think about the world today.

Thomas Downes (11)
Blaengwawr Primary School, Aberdare

Planet

P lease help, we need you
L ook around, is there any rubbish?
A nybody can recycle
N ow it is your turn to recycle
E verybody help now
T he world must be clean.

Siân Alison Smith (8)
Coedylan Primary School, Graigwen

World Environment

W alk everywhere you go
O ur planet likes to be clean
R ubbish belongs in the bin
L ove our planet, treat it with care
D on't use your wheels, use your heels!

Megan Oliver (9)
Coedylan Primary School, Graigwen

Save The Earth

S ave the Earth by putting rubbish in the bin
A ll of us can help save the Earth
V ans and cars create pollution
E arth is important, try to save it.

T ake rubbish to the tip
H elp the environment
E veryone should help.

E arth can get hot when polluted
A ny cans or rubbish can be recycled
R euse, recycle
T he world is important, help take care of it
H elp save the environment.

James Hughes (8)
Coedylan Primary School, Graigwen

Eco Code - Litter

L eave bags out to collect
I nto the recycling bags
T urn your lights off
T urn your television off after you use it
E mpty your bins and put it in bags
R ecycle your rubbish.

James Ramsay (11)
Coedylan Primary School, Graigwen

Reuse

R un to school or walk but don't go to school in a car unless you
   have to
E verybody must put their litter in the bin
U se recycled paper, not new paper
S ave our world by recycling
E verybody should try to save our world!

Tazkia Choudhury (8)
Coedylan Primary School, Graigwen

Recycle

R educe, reuse, recycle
E verybody should be helping to make the world a better place
C are for your planet
Y our planet needs help
C ar fumes cause pollution
L ove your planet
E verybody can help clean the planet by picking up litter.

Megan Davies (9)
Coedylan Primary School, Graigwen

Ecology

E verybody could make the world a better place
C lean your home
O nly walk to school and it will give you energy
L ook around to see if some things are being used
O nly recycle paper, cans and wood
G o and see if you can make the world better
Y ou can make a difference.

Leah Hallett (9)
Coedylan Primary School, Graigwen

Planet

P rotect animals and put litter in bins
L itter should be put in the bin not on the floor
A nybody can help recycle
N ot many people recycle so help
E verybody should help recycle
T ake your litter to the dump.

Lucy Thomas (8)
Coedylan Primary School, Graigwen

Planet

P ut your litter in the bin
L et's get recycling
A ll of us should put litter in a bin
N o putting litter on the floor
E arth needs our help
T hings we can recycle are boxes, cans and glass.

Rachel Birch (8)
Coedylan Primary School, Graigwen

Planet

P ut your rubbish in the bin
L ook after your home
A nyone can look after our world
N obody should throw litter on the floor
E veryone should save our planet
T idy our world!

Mali Griffiths (8)
Coedylan Primary School, Graigwen

Electricity

E nergy must be saved
L et's help save the environment
E veryone can help by walking
C ollect rubbish
T ry your best to recycle
R euse your bottles and cans
I would save if I were you
C an you help our world?
I t is better to be safe than sorry
T urn your telly off if you are not using it
Y our world, our world, everyone's world.

Kyle Rhys Adams (11), Lewis Jones & Flynn Randell (10)
Coedylan Primary School, Graigwen

Save

S olar power can save the Earth
A id the Earth by recycling your trash
V andalism is killing the Earth
E veryone has got to help by putting litter in the bin.

Joel Christian (8)
Coedylan Primary School, Graigwen

Save

S ave our planet and recycle
A ll the people on this planet help
V ery tidy people take care of our planet
E verybody save the planet now!

Jessica Howells Mullen (7)
Coedylan Primary School, Graigwen

Reuse

R ecycle your rubbish to the tip
E nough fuel-powered cars, use electronic cars instead
U se less time in the car
S ave more energy
E nough people are getting ill by the litter on the floor.

Elis Morgan Pryse (7)
Coedylan Primary School, Graigwen

Global Warming

G lobal warming can be stopped by:
L ights off when you're not in the room
O nly walk to places, don't drive
B uy only what you need to buy
A fter you use it, *recycle it*
L itter on the floor is shameful, put it in the bin

W arm, turn the heating off
A nimals can get killed from our litter so *stop*
R educe, reuse, recycle
M y computer is turned off at the plug
I hope yours is too
N ight clothes and day clothes can be given to charity
G lobal warming can stop if you follow our rules.

Chloe Davies (11) & Chloe Willetts (10)
Coedylan Primary School, Graigwen

Wind Farms

W ind makes the wind farm spin around to make electricity
I switch the lights off when we leave the house
N ever drop litter on the floor
D on't leave your charger in the plug when you're not
                                      charging something

F ollow the recycling rules
A lways pick up litter off the floor and put it in the bin
R ecycle paper that you are not using
M y mother recycles
S top throwing litter on the floor.

Lucas Hickman (10) & Joshua Powell (9)
Coedylan Primary School, Graigwen

Garden Waste

G o and pick up your litter
A lways recycle paper and cans
R euse, reduce, recycle
D irt is good for your compost heap
E arth needs your help
N ever drop your litter

W alk to school
A nd never leave the lights on
S aving energy is good for our homes
T ake care of our world
E nvironment has got to be clean.

Daniella Bedgood & Shannon Golubovic (9)
Coedylan Primary School, Graigwen

Eco-Code - Pollution

P lease don't pollute our world
O ur waste dumps are full
L itter is taking over the Earth
L and is going to be covered with rubbish
U pgrade our recycling levels
T emperatures are rising rapidly
I gnoring rubbish will kill us
O ur planet is burning
N eed a new home.

Rory McGlennon (11)
Coedylan Primary School, Graigwen

Pollution

P ollution is bad for the atmosphere
O ut goes the car, in comes the bike
L arge amounts of pollution are made every day
L et's work together to help save our planet
U se less energy every day
T o make less pollution every day
I n the air are lots of bad gases
O ut goes the light when not in use
N ever drop litter, put it in the bin.

Ben Gooding (9)
Coedylan Primary School, Graigwen

Eco-Code - Environment

E nd world pollution
N ever overuse energy
V ery small places are disappearing
I f you save energy more people will live
R educe, reuse, recycle
O pen your mind, live a better life
N ever throw away paper and plastic
M ake your recycle bag full of recyclables
E nergy is special, save it
N ever stop recycling
T ime is running out, do your part now!

Ethan Randell & Matthew Easton (10)
Coedylan Primary School, Graigwen

Eco-Code - Environment

E veryone is in this together
N obody should put an end to recycling
V anishing rainforests from far and wide
I n this changing world, things not right are happening
R ecycle and you will see a difference in the environment
O ur world's animals are disappearing every second of the day
N ations around the world are trying to reduce electricity
M illions of trees get cut down every year
E ndless rubbish is being thrown on the floor
N othing will grow if global warming carries on continuously
T errible things are happening everywhere.

Ella Bartlett-Jones & Martha Okon (10)
Coedylan Primary School, Graigwen

Eco-Code - Cut Down

C are for our environment
U se a recycling bag not a black bag
T ell people to pick up their litter

D on't drop your litter
O ne to one we have to recycle
W alk, don't waste energy
N ot many people recycle.

Jesse White (10) & Mason Ian Pritchard (9)
Coedylan Primary School, Graigwen

Litter Is Bad

L itter clutters up the planet
I put litter in the bin
T ake your rubbish to the bin
T ry to change the planet
E arth is something special, so please try to help
R ubbish can help if you put it in the bin

I think you should help
S tand up and get recycling

B ag your rubbish
A nyone can help
D rag your rubbish to the bin.

Atalya Paige Edwards (7)
Coedylan Primary School, Graigwen

Eco-Code - Global Warming

Global warming is destroying our planet.
Life is dying because we are polluting the planet.
Over the world people die.
But if we can cut down we can save the planet.
Lights are to go out when not in use.

Warming up the planet is.
All people please help us to save the planet.
Rainforests are being cut down.
Make sure you recycle and you will help our planet.
In our planet we are killing ourselves!
Not to dump rubbish in the landfill site, recycle!
Global warming is killing our planet.

Mark James (10) & Rhys Shortman (11)
Coedylan Primary School, Graigwen

Eco-Code - Rubbish

R educe waste to save our world
U se recycle bins more often
B in your food waste to keep the school clean
B ottles that are dropped are bad for the planet
I n school don't throw away rubbish
S ave our planet from waste
H elp us all to recycle.

Rhys Grainger & Ryan Alex Wheeler (10)
Coedylan Primary School, Graigwen

Save The Planet

S top using your cars so much
A ll the rubbish in the bin is better than on the streets
V ast amounts of rubbish should be recycled
E cology can help, so do your bit to save the planet

T housands of animals will die if we don't go green
H owever, we can switch to bio fuels, solar, wind power
   or hydro electricity
E liminate the use of cars and use public transport

P lenty of people could be more environmentally friendly
L ove the environment
A trocious amounts of people drive
N ever drive to school unless necessary
E rase unnecessary waste and don't buy too much
T he world might survive if we do these things.

Jocelyn Kress Churchill (9)
Coedylan Primary School, Graigwen

Save

S top dropping litter and rubbish
A ll keep the planet clean
V ery many people recycle, but some don't, so recycle
E verybody should recycle and put rubbish in the bins.

Joseph Kerslake (8)
Coedylan Primary School, Graigwen

Green

G reen, green grass across the fields
R ubbish is getting put underground, we've got to stop it
E ven if we get dirty, it is always worth it
E very place should be full of flowers
N ot a big dirty dump.

Elizabeth Wigmore (10)
Cwmbach Junior School, Aberdare

The Green Trees

The trees are so bright
And so, so green
They've always been perfect
And always been seen.

The trunk of the tree
Is brown and dark
It's nice to lean on
And it feels like the teeth of a shark

The colour is lovely
It's nice and cool
It just grows
And you don't need a tool.

Jai Mehta (9)
Cwmbach Junior School, Aberdare

Stay Green

G reen is the best colour
R educing is better than recycling
E veryone uses something again
E veryone could help the environment
N ever drop litter in this lovely world.

Owen Williams (9)
Cwmbach Junior School, Aberdare

Reduce, Reuse, Recycle! - Haikus

The trees are so green
Reduce, reuse, recycle
So there's no litter.

Do not cut down trees
Because the world won't be green
Don't cut down trees, please!

Eve Jones (9)
Cwmbach Junior School, Aberdare

Go Green Planet - Haiku

Pollution is bad
Save the trees, save the planet
Make the world happy.

Bethan Hancock (9)
Cwmbach Junior School, Aberdare

In Our Hands

What is it?
What can I see?
Oh look, it's a sign saying 3003.

So don't be mean in 3003
So stay green
The future is in our hands
So grab it while we can.

Lucy Ffion Thomas (9)
Cwmbach Junior School, Aberdare

In The Future - Green

G reen is the symbol for the environment
R euse the things from the past
E very day you can make the world a better place
E veryone can have a happy life if you recycle
N obody will have a sad life if you recycle.

Callum Lucas (10)
Cwmbach Junior School, Aberdare

Eco-Friendly - Green

G reen is for life
R euse paper to make books
E veryone could make new clothes out of old clothes
E veryone reuse shampoo bottles
N ever waste paper.

Bethan Davies (10)
Cwmbach Junior School, Aberdare

Eco-Friendly

G reen is for life
R ecycle, reduce, reuse
E co-friendly
E veryone recycles bottles
N ever waste.

Cody Bansal (8)
Cwmbach Junior School, Aberdare

Recycling

Recycling is the colour of green
It smells like fresh air
It tastes like fresh water
It feels like happiness
It sounds like birds singing
It's our future, don't throw it away.

Rhys Phillips (11)
Cwmbach Junior School, Aberdare

Hope

Hope is the colour of baby-blue
It smells like sweet roses
It tastes like a lovely Chinese meal
It sounds like birds tweeting
It feels relaxed
Hope lives in everybody
Hope be with you.

Stefan Jones (10)
Cwmbach Junior School, Aberdare

Litter

Litter is the colour of green
It tastes like feet
It smells like burning litter
It feels like muck
Litter lies in the bin.

Mitchell Griffiths (10)
Cwmbach Junior School, Aberdare

Hope

Hope is the colour of blue sky
It smells like fresh air
It tastes like cool water
It sounds like blowing trees
It feels like green grass
Hope lives with us.

Jöe Davies (10)
Cwmbach Junior School, Aberdare

Peace

Peace is the colour of bright pink
It smells like perfume
It tastes like strawberry sauce
It sounds like running water
It feels like a lovely world
Peace lives with us.

Sasiwimon Davies (10)
Cwmbach Junior School, Aberdare

Recycling

Recycling is the colour green
It smells of happiness
It tastes like chips
It feels like cotton wool
Recycling is the future.

Meirion Gratland (9)
Cwmbach Junior School, Aberdare

What Will It Be Like In 100 Years?

When you take a walk
Make sure you talk to the honeybees
Up in the trees
When you're fluttering by
Make sure you say hi to the bluebird
Watching the wind.

Rachel Kathrens (9)
Cwmbach Junior School, Aberdare

Good To Be Green

I t's good to be green because . . .
T he world would be a better place
S topping pollution puts a smile on my face

G od made our world to be a safe land
O f people and animals hand in hand
O h mercy, pleads the Earth's core
D ie will I at the crack of dawn

T oday we can make tomorrow last
O f the dreaded memories of the past

B e gone all the smoke of the polluted sky
E very animal is left to die

G o away all the litter
R ound each corner when I see you, it makes my mouth taste bitter
E veryone prepare to get ready
E veryone get steady
N ow is the time to save the world.

Jake Falcon (11)
Cwmbach Junior School, Aberdare

Climate Change

C ould you help save the planet and yourself?
L ife could stop
I f you use the 3 Rs you could save the planet
M aybe you don't know what to do
A ll of you can help
T he climate is changing and you could stop it
E ven if it is just a little

C an you buy and use a recycling bin?
H anging on a string our future is
A ll you have to do is wash at 30 degrees
N ow we are at a critical point
G o and do something, we have to
E ven you could do your bit.

Owain Evans (10)
Cwmbach Junior School, Aberdare

Recycle

Think about the future
Think about the past
Think about the present
If you want this world to last.

Think about the sunshine
Think about the grass
Think about recycling
When you recycle glass . . .

Callum Quinn & Thomas (11)
Cwmbach Junior School, Aberdare

Go Green

Reduce, reuse and recycle
Fish need clean water
Animals breathe clean air
The ozone layer is getting damaged
Pollution must stop!

Rhobet Bull & Kristian Enoch (11)
Cwmbach Junior School, Aberdare

Our World!

Our world today is beginning to be a wreck
So if you want to help make a change
Then listen to my words.

It's our world, one planet
Don't let it rot away
Let's keep our world for our children
Let's keep our planet okay.

Georgia Louise Davies (11)
Cwmbach Junior School, Aberdare

The World Is Green

T he grass is lovely and green
H iking is the way to get fit
E co is to save our planet

W alking is a way to get fit
O rienteering round the world
R ecycle your rubbish
L itter is rubbish, so pick it up
D o not throw your litter in the bin, recycle it.

Kiera James (10)
Cwmbach Junior School, Aberdare

War Must End!

W ill war end?
A ll war is bad
R eally bad things happen in war

M en are dying every day, they are throwing their lives away
U nless we put an end to war, war will put an end to us
S top it now, stop it for good
T omorrow's children will be good

E veryone will die
N othing will exist
D on't take part in war!

Cory Thomas (11)
Cwmbach Junior School, Aberdare

Earth Is Dying

E arth is dying, let's make it better
A ll I have to do is send this letter
R ainforests are going down
T he Earth in return gets a frown
H ave you tried to make it worse?

I f you do you'll get a curse
S top with cars on the road

D o not use it to reload
Y ou can help, please just do
I n the eco-helping zoo
N ow go and tell your friends
G iving you an eco-lend.

Jack Harris (11)
Cwmbach Junior School, Aberdare

Recycle Today

R ecycling can save the world
E ven when you don't know you have
C ars drive everywhere, giving off pollution
Y et, children don't know
C leaners clean roads of rubbish
L eaving nothing there
E ven taking stuff you can recycle

T oday we can still recycle
O nly not many people
D o what they should do
A fter people take the rubbish
Y ou wonder if it was a good idea.

Deiniol Llewellyn (10)
Cwmbach Junior School, Aberdare

Green World

G reen world is a happy world
R educe is the first of the 3 Rs
E at healthy food
E veryone should try it
N o one will regret it

W ill you try to help us too?
O r our world will be unhappy
R educe, reuse, recycle is easy to follow
L ook after our world
D o your bit to save our planet!

Zoe Jayne Jones (10)
Cwmbach Junior School, Aberdare

Eco Time

E is for recycling
C an't have everyone wasting things
O nly tiny things are what you need to do

T ime for everyone to
I nherit the idea
M ake recycling a habit
E veryone can help.

Sean Williams (11)
Cwmbach Junior School, Aberdare

Eco-Man

I am the eco-man
I make things better
I will lend a helping hand
But only if it will help you understand

We want to stop pollution
But the world is a big place
But if we work together
We could work at a quick pace.

James Williams (11)
Cwmbach Junior School, Aberdare

Save The Animals

Animals are dying each and every day
By cutting all the rainforests down, we throw their lives away
We have got to save the animals' homes
Before long there won't be anything left, just bones.

So please will you help us, it will really mean a lot
None of this will fade away or never be forgot
If you're wondering how
To save the animals now
Just make this your environmental vow
We have got to save the planet
Make this your habit.

Abbie Kate Jones & Emily Watts (11)
Cwmbach Junior School, Aberdare

The Help From The Big Green Poetry Machine

The trouble with the environment these days
Is that there's people throwing waste away
And also people are making fun of others
Because they don't look the same as you
But the Big Green Poetry Machine has come
To make the world a better place
So here are some things that you can do
And if you do it, we'll help you too.

Don't drive your kids to school
It makes pollution and it's not cool
Say no to litter, it's just a waste
Reuse, reduce, recycle
It makes the world a better place
Stop making fun of people that are different to you
They're no different than any of us.

Now you've heard what we want you to do
We hope you're going to make the world a better place
Remember these things that we've said
Because you can put it into someone else's head
And in a few years you'll be saying
That was really worth doing.

But also you've got to plant some things
Like daffodils, poppies, all kinds of plants
And we will thank you for doing this
You will carry on doing these things
And you might grow up to be an eco-teacher
And teach the other children to make things better.

Connor Llewellyn (11)
Cwmbach Junior School, Aberdare

Litter

Litter, litter
On the ground
The grass is green
The floor is brown
Everyone can see
The littering that you have done.

Litter, litter
On the ground
Why do you throw it there?
Please don't turn your face
Put your rubbish in the right place.

Nia Davie (10)
Gurnos CP School, Swansea

Pollution

Pollution is bad because it affects the atmosphere
So don't drop your rubbish here
Walk to school it means you use less fuel
So using less fuel means cleaner air
And that shows how much we care
It's important to recycle to save our planet
So recycle your cans, bottles and papers
And don't forget to tell your neighbours
This planet is the only one we've got
So we must not forget to take care of it a lot.

James Moore (11)
Gurnos CP School, Swansea

The Big Green Thing

Don't throw it away
You don't have to pay
To recycle your stuff
It wouldn't make you huff and puff
It's just not fair
When people don't care
So recycle your old top
And just walk to the shop.

Abbie Lodwick (10)
Gurnos CP School, Swansea

Sweet As Tulip

Our world is like a shooting star
It smells as sweet as a tulip
It tastes like a birthday cake
It could sound as happy as a cheer
But it's like a bank robbery
Stabbed with a knife
It cannot breathe because of its stifling death
The Earth's skin is rotten like an apple
The Earth is sad and wants to live
It calls to us for help
It cries but we don't hear
If it could have one wish
It would be to be looked after like a child.

Tamzin Davies (8)
Maindee Primary School, Newport

Only One World

Our world is like a magical orb
It could smell as sweet as a red rose
It could be as delicious as water
It could sound as happy as Heaven's angel
But it is like a devil's nightmare, dark and dank
It feels like a scorpion has stung it
It cannot breathe because of pollution
The Earth is dried and wasted
It calls out to us but we don't care to notice
It cries to us but we take no heed
If the Earth could have one wish
It would be no more hurt or pain.

Mahida Rahman (8)
Maindee Primary School, Newport

Rotten World

Our world is like a bunch of flowers
It could sound as happy as scoring a goal
But it's like I'm having a nightmare
It feels like I'm bad, it cannot breathe
Because the air is bad
The skin is rotten
The Earth is sad and wants to scream
It calls out to us but we don't hear
It is cruel
If it could have one wish
It would be water to drink.

Callum Shaw (9)
Maindee Primary School, Newport

Our Planet

Our world is like a beautiful butterfly
It could smell as sweet as blossom
It could taste as good as honey on toast
It could sound as happy as a winning team scoring a goal
It could sound like laughter in space
But it's like a rotten bird
It feels like a growing rash
It cannot breathe because of poisonous gas in the air
The Earth's skin is covered with cuts and bruises
The Earth is sad and wants to run away
It cries, but we stand there and laugh
If it could have one wish it would be to be cherished.

Suhayb Tariq (9)
Maindee Primary School, Newport

The Planet Is Crying

Our world is like a rose with no thorns
It could smell as sweet as magnolia
It could taste as good as a sweet cherry
It could sound as happy as nature growing
It could taste as good as a sweet cherry
It could sound as happy as nature growing
But it's like an erupting volcano
It feels like pins hurting the Earth
It cannot breathe because of pollution
The Earth's skin is rough as bark
The Earth is sad and wants to be left alone
It calls out to us but we disobey
It cries out but we turn our heads
If it could have one wish it would be less pollution.

Rita Mwanza (9)
Maindee Primary School, Newport

Make The World A Better Place

Make the world a better place
Remove your footprint from its face
All the poverty, war and litter
Makes our world seem so, so bitter
All the disease and pollution
There must be some solution
Rainforests being cut down
Come on trees, stand up proud
Recycle, recycle and do a little bit more
It makes our world seem so less sore!

Eleanor Baker (10)
Pembroke Dock Community School, Pembroke Dock

Recycling

Our world is such a precious place
We have to slow down our very fast pace
We need to recycle, reuse, reduce you see
These are the 3 Rs of ecology
I want to grow up in a clean environment
So please listen to this very
Important statement!

Holly Adams (11)
Pembroke Dock Community School, Pembroke Dock

Recycling

R ecycling is important
E veryone can help
C yclones are attacking
Y ou can stop this
'C ause we are destroying
L itter is important
I t causes pollution
N othing is as important as
G etting our world clean.

Marcus Blair (11)
Pembroke Dock Community School, Pembroke Dock

War's Here

People dying
Parents are trying
To stop kids crying

Homes are destroyed
People annoyed
Lives destroyed

Bombs are defused
Children confused
Parents cannot reuse

We can mend
Or even send
Our troops to defend.

Amy Goodman (11)
Pembroke Dock Community School, Pembroke Dock

Disease

Oh no, the tribes are getting diseases
The government say, 'Oh, it's just a cough and sneeze!'
But it's more than that
They're slowly getting skinny
And America and Britain are getting fat!

People are dying every five seconds
In that time you could buy a burger I reckon
Maybe sometimes we should see
What good lives we have
Where some people's main course is tree!

We were the ones who should have left them in peace
Now we have given them terrible disease!

Lucy Hearn (11)
Pembroke Dock Community School, Pembroke Dock

The Environment

Pollution is a nasty state in the seas which hurts the animals.
Pollution is a nasty thing especially on the fields as when they fly by
It gets caught up in the bags.
Pollution is effective in the oceans too, the garbage goes into the seas
And also from the loo.

Recycling can help, paper, wrappers too,
Did I mention packets and sometimes plastic too?

Extinction with the animals affects our lives as well,
Fish for food,
Sharks for teeth
And also tiger skin.
Elephants for their tusks
And many others too.

What happens with diseases?
Pneumonia from cold weather
And also deadly flu
And if we keep on littering, the plague will affect us too.

Jake Evans (11)
Pembroke Dock Community School, Pembroke Dock

Recycle A Little More

We need to make the world a better place
To live, eat and sleep
So listen now, it's time to see
The world is a litter machine
We can all just do a little bit more
To recycle at home
If we all recycle a little bit more
We can all have more
More life
More air
More animals to see
Our homes and world are a big machine
A litter dustbin you can see
So *recycle* a little bit more
No angry face anymore!

Chloe Cardy (11)
Pembroke Dock Community School, Pembroke Dock

Don't Ruin Our World

In the Amazon Rainforest, where animals live
In their habitats where they survive
People came and cut down trees
Including ones with a beehive
We're losing oxygen on our planet
So, then we must be insane
Species are lost, trees are cut down
Not a lot remain.

If you get some rubbish and throw it away
It may go into the sea
Pollution is caused, dirty water is made
With rust, metal and mercury
Sea creatures get an underwater asthma
And soon, sadly, they die
Oxygen's lost from the sea to the air
Not much is left in the sky.

Being homeless, poverty and war too
Litter and disease is made
Pollution, extinction and many more
Some people could catch the plague
Leave litter in a corner, for it to stay
Then it gets all curled
And so I say, recycle, don't litter
And then . . .
You won't ruin our world!

Rhys James (10)
Pembroke Dock Community School, Pembroke Dock

Help You And Me

Keep grass green
Keep the lakes clean
For you and me

Stop diseases for people like you and me
Stop war for the poor and for you and me

Keep the litter from the weaker
And from you and me
Help stop pollution, homelessness, war, disease
Litter and many more
So for your sake, please, for me
You and the world.

Ryan Edwards (11)
Pembroke Dock Community School, Pembroke Dock

Recycle Now

R emember the community needs to be clean
E ven the countryside too
C oke and cans, trash and sweets
Y ou must be tidy to our community
C lean our local parks and our streets
L eaving trash on our streets harms young animals
E nough to kill them. Now stop and think before you throw trash into
                                                                    our streets

N ow even your garden has to be tidy
O n our streets now there's no trash to be seen
W hen we children walk onto the streets
   We're pleased with the beautiful sight they see!

Emily Pyle
Pembroke Dock Community School, Pembroke Dock

Litter

L itter, litter everywhere
I can't stand the mess
T oo many people throwing their rubbish
T oo much of a smell
E very day people see rubbish which they don't like
R ats will eat it.

Ffion Howells (9)
Pembroke Dock Community School, Pembroke Dock

Litter

Litter, litter everywhere
It is as horrible as can be
I can't take it anymore
I think my head is going to explode
The Earth will soon be a big ball of litter
So don't throw rubbish anymore
Please don't!

Ben Lascelles (9)
Pembroke Dock Community School, Pembroke Dock

Litter

L ook at the litter on the floor, smashed glass everywhere
I would like you to use the bin to put your litter in
T he broken glass is hurting animals
T he rats are trying to get into the bin
E very day someone is throwing litter on the floor
R ight now my friends will stop being a litter bug.

Craig Jones (9)
Pembroke Dock Community School, Pembroke Dock

Litter

L itter on the floor
I sn't it disgusting?
T oo lazy to put it in the recycling bin
T he rats are coming to eat the horrible litter
E very day the Earth is getting messier
R ows of empty bins.

Daniel Hearn (8)
Pembroke Dock Community School, Pembroke Dock

Litter

L itter on the floor and in your garden
I sn't it smelly?
T he animals are in danger
T his is our chance to save them
E ach day animals are dying
R ows of rubbish piled on the floor.

Shauna Brereton (9)
Pembroke Dock Community School, Pembroke Dock

Litter

L itter is everywhere
I sn't it dangerous?
T oo much litter on the street
T oo many people are dropping litter
E veryone is dropping rubbish on the floor
R un and pick up the rubbish.

Shannon Howells (9)
Pembroke Dock Community School, Pembroke Dock

Litter

L itter on the floor
I n the floor more and more
T oo much rubbish on a ball
T oo many people fall
E veryone is dying
R ubbish in the river killing our wildlife.

Derek Brundrett (8)
Pembroke Dock Community School, Pembroke Dock

Litter

Litter, litter everywhere
Litter all around
Litter should be put in the bin
Where it is found
I can't stand the disgrace
Of litter lying all around.

Ryan Bourner (9)
Pembroke Dock Community School, Pembroke Dock

Wartime

W ar is dying, people are crying
A bomb is falling, it's crashing again
R eading the news, people dying
T he war has started, they're killing again
I wish the war would stop again and again
M en are risking their lives for others
E veryone is cheering because the war is all over.

MJ Morgan (10)
Pembroke Dock Community School, Pembroke Dock

Nature

Nature is everywhere from rainforests to animals
And they're all dying so here's some things you should do.

Dig a hole, plant a tree and then you'll see
How pretty a tree can be
Animals and extinction, why now?
It's like flushing a goldfish down the loo
Why is this so easy to do?

So now you know what to do
So let's make the world better for you.

Luke Hawkins (10)
Pembroke Dock Community School, Pembroke Dock

The Rainforest

Trees are dying because of us.
Use less paper and that will help.
So if we reuse the paper
That means we are helping,
So we should.
Please just help a little bit,
Remember the three Rs.

Elle Davenport (11)
Pembroke Dock Community School, Pembroke Dock

Destroying The Rainforest

R ainforests are being cut down
A nimals are left homeless
I n the rainforest animals are homeless
N ow we must recycle and give their homes back
F orests are being destroyed
O h please, stop logging and building roads
R un away Amerindians, they're coming
E veryone help to stop, people are destroying the rainforest,
only 70% remains
S tart helping people to rebuild the rainforest
T ry to help people build homes for the poor please
Help now!

James Richard Beynon (11)
Pembroke Dock Community School, Pembroke Dock

Rainforest Destruction

The rainforest is in terrible danger
The beautiful animals don't stand anymore
They have no homes to go to sleep in
Because we are destroying the nature
Their homes are not there to live in
We must stop this destruction right now
The people are dying
The plants will not grow
We must save the rainforest or it will die
Please people, be big and green.

Ben Veal (10)
Pembroke Dock Community School, Pembroke Dock

Going Green

G oing green is not hard
O ur rainforest is being destroyed
I love all the animals
N o one is helping
G ive people their homes back

G oing green, everyone can do it
R ead a booklet about it
E veryone is helping
E vil people are destroying it
N obody can stop it now they are all dying.

Ashton Scott (11)
Pembroke Dock Community School, Pembroke Dock

War!

H elp the environment
E nvironment is safe
L ights are flashing
M en are coming again
E veryone is frightened
T he war is starting again!

Liam Gammer (11)
Pembroke Dock Community School, Pembroke Dock

Pollution

Please, please save the world
Keep the trees and beaches
From going
Please, please help us to
Stop pollution and rubbish from
Pushing the animals to extinction
Please, please keep the world tidy

Please people, please people
Help us to keep the world tidy
And go really green.

George Hancock (11)
Pembroke Dock Community School, Pembroke Dock

The Rainforest

People are dying
No medicine for them
Disease all around
Trees are being cut
Nowhere for the animals or people to live
Please help us, do your bit.

Alicia Kingdom (10)
Pembroke Dock Community School, Pembroke Dock

Animals Of The Rainforest

Animals are lovely
People think they're cute
Please don't abuse them
They are one of us
They are getting killed
No thanks to us.

Jack Jamie Dow (11)
Pembroke Dock Community School, Pembroke Dock

Animals Of The Rainforest

Animals are loving
Don't you think they're cute?
And trees are being cut, only 7% remain
The animals are being killed
I feel terrible and you know you do too.

Tawny Davies (12)
Pembroke Dock Community School, Pembroke Dock

The Dying Rainforest

The rainforest's dying
When we are lying doing nothing about it
The habitats are going
So we can have wood
We need to save the rainforest
If we don't we will have no oxygen
In the future there may never be a rainforest
Help us save the rainforest!

Kayley Davies (11)
Pembroke Dock Community School, Pembroke Dock

War

Bombs are flying
People are dying
All around the town.
Why are we falling down?
Hopefully the end is in sight.
Why do we have to fight?

Jordan Wright (11)
Pembroke Dock Community School, Pembroke Dock

Save Our World

Save our world
Look after our rainforests
Don't cut down our trees
Or we'll lose our animals.
People are destroying our environment
Because they want to make roads
Don't pollute our cities
By throwing rubbish
Just because you don't like where we live
You might not realise but
You're destroying our environment.

Matthew Veal (11)
Pembroke Dock Community School, Pembroke Dock

War Is Coming

War is coming
Don't be afraid
We must fight
We must, we must
Fight to the death
Guns, men and torches
We find on death row.

Leigh Jenkins (10)
Pembroke Dock Community School, Pembroke Dock

Litter

L itter should be in bins, not on the floor
I 'll help you and you help me
T ell people to pick up their rubbish
T ell people to pick up rubbish for the world
E very day put the rubbish in the bin please
R ubbish should go in the bin, not on the ground, please.

Katherine Brookes (11)
Pembroke Dock Community School, Pembroke Dock

War

In a war, everyone is killing
A lot of blood spilling and spilling
Not everyone is willing
So stop the war and have
Peace!

Billy Kilpatrick (10)
Pembroke Dock Community School, Pembroke Dock

Respect

Respect is very important to me
I respect my friends and my family
If we all respect one another
We might learn to like each other
People are different, yes it's true
Black and white, me and you
Let's stop fighting, let's get along
Come on everybody, let's sing a song
But there's one more thing I nearly forgot
Look after our Earth, so it doesn't get hot
We don't want storms and we don't want flood
We don't want our Earth covered in mud
We can save the planet, yes we can
You don't want to catch that much of a tan.

Eden Statham (8)
Pengelli Primary School, Swansea

The Three Rs

You can recycle all sorts of things
Like paper, glass, cans, clothes and plastic
Recycling means you can use them again and again and again
What do you want our world to be like?
A *big* rubbish dump or a beautiful world of nature?
Throw your rubbish away because rubbish doesn't throw itself away
Please use the three Rs
Reduce, reuse and recycle.

Josh Hier (9)
Pengelli Primary School, Swansea

Litter Bugs

The rubbish swirls around my feet
This makes the environment look un-neat
The parks are littered with bottles and cans
Why can't they use the bins?
Come on guys, let's clean up now
You've seen the adverts so you all know how!

Francesca Anne Oak (9)
Pengelli Primary School, Swansea

Living In The City

Traffic jams
Car fumes
Noisy workmen
Mixing hot smelly tar factory
Fumes polluting the air
And lighting up the sky
Litter everywhere
Please recycle
Please recycle
I wish I lived in the country!

Cameron Davey (8)
Pengelli Primary School, Swansea

Keeping The World Green

G o green
R ecycle
E nvironmentally friendly
E nergy efficient
N ature is important.

Rhiannon Bevan (8)
Pengelli Primary School, Swansea

Save Our Planet

S ummer, winter, spring and autumn are our four seasons
E ach season has different weather
A ll of us drive too many cars which give off fumes
S o all our seasons are now like one because the
O zone layer has a hole in it
N ow we have to work together to
S top all the fumes. Walk and cycle!

Ben Thomas (7)
Pengelli Primary School, Swansea

Environment

E verybody should recycle
N ever leave your rubbish on the street
V ehicles, use them less
I wish I could do more
R educe, reuse and recycle
O ur planet needs us like
N ever before so
M ake changes now
E very little helps
N ot tomorrow but
T oday.

Courtney Lauren Huxtable (9)
Pengelli Primary School, Swansea

A Solution For Pollution

A solution for pollution
Reuse, reclaim, recycle
Leave the car, take your bicycle
Litter is bitter, don't leave it lying around
It makes such a mess
And flowers can't be found
The birds and animals are really pretty
We like to see them in our city
Think of the planet before you make a move
A solution for pollution, stay in the groove!

Chloë O'Hare (9)
Pengelli Primary School, Swansea

No More Litter, Keep Green

Litter, litter everywhere
People just don't seem to care
Throwing rubbish in our streets
Making it a rubbish heap.

Stop this litter or beware
We need more bins everywhere
Parks are clean, our roads will gleam
No more litter, let's be green!

Cerys-Jade Hickman (8)
Pengelli Primary School, Swansea

Green

Green is the colour of the grass
Green is the colour of the leaves on a tree
Green is the colour we all should be
To keep our world nice and clean.

David Ashley Symonds (7)
Pengelli Primary School, Swansea

Recycle, Recycle

Leaves are green, grass is green
Start recycling and you won't be mean
Recycle, recycle, it's the best thing to do
Don't let the polar bears live in a zoo.

Joe Davies (8)
Pengelli Primary School, Swansea

The Fall Of The Forest

We stand up tall
Our backs all straight
Many arms outstretched
Our palms turned up
We hide the forest animals from friend and foe alike
Alas, out time is almost up
We live in constant fear
As Man forgets how much the eco-system relies on what we offer.

Liam Oak (11)
Pengelli Primary School, Swansea

A Better Place

The world would be a better place
If people put their rubbish in the correct place
Recycle, recycle, that's what they should do
Then the world would be a better place for me and you.

Chloe Harding (10)
Pengelli Primary School, Swansea

Animal Planet

Animals, animals everywhere
Do you think us children care?
But we show you that we do
Just by visiting the zoo
Here we learn about you too.

The ice is melting in the Arctic
Polar bear is feeling sad
What can I do to help this bear?
Tell my dad to get off his chair.

Don't take us to school in the car
Let us walk, it's not that far.

Sara Piper (8)
Pengelli Primary School, Swansea

Oh Earth

Oh Earth, oh Earth
You precious sphere
The people are building
The end is near
Oh Earth, oh Earth
The trees are going
We're trying to help
As we are growing
Oh Earth, oh Earth
You need us to care
To show that we're willing
To clean up your air
Oh Earth, oh Earth
You precious sphere
The children are helping
So don't shed a tear.

Ciaran Foley (9)
Pengelli Primary School, Swansea

Solution For Pollution

In our world there is pollution.
Please be part of the solution.
The problem's big and hard to solve
But will help our world revolve.
Think of what you can recycle
Not use your car but walk or cycle.
We cut our trees, whole forests gone
Yet no one thought that it was wrong.
With all the animals gone to waste
Too much damage, we must make haste.
Reuse it twice and don't be mean
All will help to keep it green.

Callum Davies (8)
Pengelli Primary School, Swansea

Litter

Litter, litter everywhere
I hate litter
It makes me despair
Paper, plastic, thrown around
It all looks like a very big mound
No one uses the bins
People should recycle things.

Millie Baker (10)
Pengelli Primary School, Swansea

Do We Care?

Guns get fired
Bombs explode
Lives are lost
Houses destroyed
Men and women die
For our own interests
Trenches are dug
Bullets whizz past
Sometimes I wonder, do we care?

Aneurin Donald (11)
Pengelli Primary School, Swansea

Homeless People

Why are people homeless?
Why does it make me sad?
How come I am so helpless?
Maybe I should ask my dad
Everybody needs a home
We need a place to stay
A place to have a good play
It really makes me groan
When people don't have a home.

Nicole Clark
Pengelli Primary School, Swansea

The Environment

The sun is shining, the grass is green
The sea is blue, we are all happy
I hope you are too.

But that will all change one day
The sun won't shine
There will be no grass
The sea will be gone if you don't change
The world will change
Make a difference
Do something now
This is everyone's world!

Daisy South
Pengelli Primary School, Swansea

Our World

Ten plastic bottles, not in recycling
Nine environments, all polluted
Eight rainforests, all chopped down
Seven cars with smoky fumes
Six children, all in poverty
Five families who have no food
Four animals, living in danger
Three people trying to help
Two bins filled with litter
One world, our only one
We all need to help!

Jade Harriet Evans-Hope (9)
Rhayader Primary School, Rhayader

Can We Help?

I heard the birds tweeting and eating their last bits of food
I saw some people living on the street
Homes have gone, they're left alone
Diseases spreading to people and animals
No doctors to help
The noisy war, a danger to people and animals
Let the world be still, let there be peace
Can we help our world?

Hana Albiston (8)
Rhayader Primary School, Rhayader

Pollution

P ollution kills animals, trees and planets
O ne of the worst kinds is acid rain and gas
L ots of different kinds of pollution
L oads of people need to help
U nlucky countries are full of pollution
T ry and stop pollution
I need people to stop polluting
O nly one world, so don't pollute it
N ow do something about it!

Rupert Storer (9)
Rhayader Primary School, Rhayader

Animals Are Becoming Extinct

Animals are becoming extinct
There are about 20,000 animal types left
Ones in danger are nearly all gone
Some have been poisoned
Some have been killed
Now they are nearly all extinct
What are you going to do?

Courtney Price (9)
Rhayader Primary School, Rhayader

Recycle Now

R ecycling is good for the world
E nvironments need recycling
C an you help our world by recycling?
Y our world is in danger
C ans and bottles need to be recycled
L ove the world with all your heart
E veryone needs to help

N o excuses to stop recycling
O pportunities for recycling everywhere
W hat are you waiting for? (Recycle now!)

Breanna Joy Downey (9)
Rhayader Primary School, Rhayader

Save The Rainforests

The rainforests are getting smaller, smaller and smaller
The Amazon in Brazil and the rainforests in the world
                                                             are getting smaller
If nobody cuts them down there will be less suffering
The tree animals won't get harmed
If they get chopped down there will be less oxygen to breathe
You don't need paper from wood because you can recycle.

Jacob Sylvester (9)
Rhayader Primary School, Rhayader

Making The World A Better Place

The rainforests are getting smaller, which is making me sad
Having war is making me mad.

We can stop the rainforests being cut down by recycling paper
We can't stop war, from killing people
We want to stop the rainforests being cut down quicker, but we can't.

We also want to stop war but sadly we can't
We all want to stop these things happening
We can only stop one which is very sad!

Toby Lewis (9)
Rhayader Primary School, Rhayader

Extinction

A lways look after animals
N ever ruin their habitats
I mportant animals shouldn't be killed
M ake the world a better place
A nimals deserve to live
L eave them alone
S tay away from wild ones.

Rebecca Findley (8)
Rhayader Primary School, Rhayader

People Don't Realise What They Are Doing

Monkeys are ill
Birds are shot
Tigers are beaten
Soon animals will all be extinct
Some don't have food
Some are left alone
Some are very ill
People don't realise what they are doing
Rubbish left on streets
Bottles are left on roads
Packets are used and left
People aren't using bins
People don't realise what they are doing.

Nicole Williams (9)
Rhayader Primary School, Rhayader

Rainforests

In the rainforest
Animals are suffering
Because of people
Animals will be extinct
So please don't cut down the trees.

Reece Ware (11)
St Mary's Junior School, Caldicot

Litter

Lying on the streets
Rotting day by day
Stinking, smelly and nasty
Please put litter in the bin
Or you'll destroy our planet!

Melissa Blenkiron (11)
St Mary's Junior School, Caldicot

Animals And Extinction

The fox is dying
People are shooting them all
Not many are left
Trying to escape the traps
But being caught and bleeding.

Chloe Bryant (11)
St Mary's Junior School, Caldicot

War

Death and homelessness
Fires from all the huge bombs
And pollution too
Threat of nuclear weapons
And slaves and sacrifices.

Joseph Russ (11)
St Mary's Junior School, Caldicot

Rainforests

Animals are trapped
Habitats fading away
Homeless animals
Rainforests are vanishing
The rainforests are dying.

Daniel Gates (11)
St Mary's Junior School, Caldicot

Racism

Racism is bad
Black and white people are mad
This upsets people
People have favouritism
Racism makes people sad.

Nia Leonard (11)
St Mary's Junior School, Caldicot

Litter

Litter goes in bins
Litter causes pollution
Litter is smelly
Litter causes diseases
Come on, let's keep Earth
Tidy!

Katy Hunt (11)
St Mary's Junior School, Caldicot

Poverty

Sitting on the street
As poverty has its way
Hungry and lonely
Living in cardboard houses
Very poor and very sad.

Thomas James Hulme (10)
St Mary's Junior School, Caldicot

Help Our Animals - Haiku

Help our animals
Their lives will be much better
If you recycle.

Meaghan Rowe (7)
St Mary's Junior School, Caldicot

Recycle Today - Haiku

Save the animals
Recycle your trash today
Please make an effort.

Chloe Woodman (8)
St Mary's Junior School, Caldicot

Save Us - Haiku

Save animals' lives
Love our big environment
Always recycle!

Abigail Green (8)
St Mary's Junior School, Caldicot

Polar Bears - Haiku

Earth getting hotter
Ice melts and polar bears die
Help save their lives, *now!*

Kelly Hooper (8)
St Mary's Junior School, Caldicot

Help The Rainforest - Haiku

I live here you know
Please do not cut the trees down
Recycle instead.

Shanice Taaffe (8)
St Mellons CW Primary School, Llanrumney

Rainforests

Loud, noisy animals
As happy as can be
Until the humans come along
And cut down the trees.

Big tall trees
Are feeling very sad
For not recycling paper
Is very, very bad.

Joanne Hares (9)
St Mellons CW Primary School, Llanrumney

Trees In The Rainforest - Haiku

One sunny morning
I was chopped down by an axe
Stop this happening.

Chloe Thomas (8)
St Mellons CW Primary School, Llanrumney

Rainforest

Recycle more to save the trees
Reduce and reuse your paper please
Help the trees grow to great heights
Save the rainforest with all your might.

Use recycled paper more and more
Please don't waste it anymore
Listen to my advice Sir
Don't buy coats with real fur.

Things made from horn and ivory
Will take the forest away from you and me
So let's act now, don't waste time
Thank you for listening to my rhyme.

Hannah Graves (8)
St Mellons CW Primary School, Llanrumney

The Rainforest

The rainforest is alive
The tall trees are swishing in the breeze
The leaves are like their hair
The branches are their hands
Grabbing, grabbing, grabbing
Dancing, dancing to the music of the birds
The amazing colourful flowers are opening up
To the blue sky as the rain is crashing down.

Jack Voyle (8)
St Mellons CW Primary School, Llanrumney

The Rainforest

The rainforest is alive
The tall trees are swishing in the breeze
The leaves are like their hair
The branches are their hands
Grabbing, grabbing, grabbing
Dancing, dancing to the music of the birds
The amazing colourful flowers
Are opening up to the blue sky
As the rain is crashing down.

Jake Morgan (9)
St Mellons CW Primary School, Llanrumney

Litter - Cinquain

Listen
Do not put it
On the floor. Stop and think!
Reduce what you use in your house
Reduce!

William Adams (9)
St Mellons CW Primary School, Llanrumney

Recycle

Recycle it, recycle it
It's easy as can be
Get all of your clothes out
And give them to charity
Don't get new bags from Tesco
Reuse and reuse, make the mess go!

Ieuan Burridge-Bryant (8)
St Mellons CW Primary School, Llanrumney

Rainforests

I am a lonely dark tree
With flowers and leaves
A wet hot plant
In a dark forest
A lonely sad animal lives in me
So don't chop me down
And help to save the forest
Help to recycle more.

Alicia Feneck (9)
St Mellons CW Primary School, Llanrumney

Rainforest

I am a lonely dark tree
With flowers and leaves
A wet hot plant
In a dark forest
A lonely sad animal lives in me
So do not chop me down
And help save forests
Help to recycle more.

Bryony Thomas (8)
St Mellons CW Primary School, Llanrumney

Untitled

A very small planet, green and blue
But it is very beautiful
And it is called planet Earth
Where you can make discoveries
On creatures and very relaxing water
With no chemicals in the seas
Fresh food and alive trees
In the rainforest
And extremely rare animals that live longer
And lovely dragonflies that love to fly
And in canyons with birds that fly over lofting high
Cute reptiles like a spiky devil and a humungous dragon
Lions that roar as loud as horns
Do not destroy the planet, you're lucky to be alive
So treat the Earth as you would like to be treated.

Joshua McConnell (10)
St Monica's CW Primary School, Heath

A Recipe For A Greener Planet

The planet should look like a beautiful, nice, astonishing, lovely,
>green place

That's really colourful, so now I'll give you the recipe
To make your world a better, spotless, round world.

Ingredients for the recipe:
Get some recycled rubbish and mash it all together
Add some cool, curvy, cold compost
With some vicious, vile, vertical vegetables
But last but not least winning, wiggly worms
And there you have your ingredients
So now our world is a much more beautiful place.

Stop littering and start recycling paper
To make our great, green world
Then there you have a better place to live.

Jamil Alam (9)
St Monica's CW Primary School, Heath

A Recipe For A Greener Planet

Gather caring, kind people and take them outside and clean up
                                                      the dirty old town
Take the caring and kind people out into the countryside
And cut the crops and start watering the woolly, wet, cotton plants
Take the group and start to grow grass and crops on the city centre
And make posters and put the pretty posters in windows
Lots of people gathered in the city centre
Make an announcement and say come with me and save
                                                      the big blue planet
Gather the oils and gases in the city and store it in the garage
By my house, so no one can use it
Let the people use water for the cars and use lunch boxes
                                                      for all the fruity food
Make people want to stop littering
Make people want to love their big blue planet
We should look after our big blue planet
Get the group and take them back to the town
See if everything has grown and chop or dice them
Ask if people want to grow and stir a lawn
Write a letter to me or my group saying I want to grow a lawn
They can join our organisation
Save our big blue planet
Put it in the bin, not on the floor.

Lily Richards (10)
St Monica's CW Primary School, Heath

A recipe For A Greener Planet

Take a couple of months
Clean them through of all rubbish
In our world and make it a green, clean fighting machine.

Add your ingredients:
Get some compost
And get some rubbish
Throw it in the bin
Get some lovely, mouldy, fat;
Fluffy, fantastic fruit
Put it in the compost bin
And now you've got a lovely soil
And you can grow green, great grass.

Now the world is a better place to live.

Patrick Jolly (9)
St Monica's CW Primary School, Heath

Untitled

Recycle your rubbish, it's killing our world
Get kind caring people, cut polluting the world

Get a compost pile
Mix it with fruit and vegetable peels
Make the world a greener place.

Get out of your shiny car
Get on your bike
It stops gas ruining our world.

If you stop we will have a better planet
You can have clear blue seas
Green land with no rubbish
That would be amazing
So stop chopping down our trees.

Kesia Osborne (10)
St Monica's CW Primary School, Heath

Toxic Nightmare!

Rubbish, rubbish everywhere
We can stop a toxic nightmare
Don't drop litter
Make the world a better place
Don't drop litter
It's a big disgrace
respect your environment
Respect the Earth
Respect the planet
For all it's worth!

Benjamin Caffell (8)
Trelewis Primary School, Merthyr Tydfil

Recycling Rap

Care for your planet
Respect, respect
Recycle your waste
It's better, better
Reuse your rubbish
It's cleaner, cleaner
Don't throw it on the floor
Dirty, dirty
Can it be reused?
Think, think
Hurry up and do it
Now, now
Come on and do it
Yeah, yeah!

Thomas Matthews (8)
Trelewis Primary School, Merthyr Tydfil

C'Mon Everyone!

Have you thought of going in the streets and seeing the rubbish
that you eat?
If you see some pick it up, give the world some good luck
Rubbish will overflow some day, so try and help the world today
Please help the planet, c'mon everyone, it's the whole job done
Will you help the planet?
Will you help the planet?
Thank you very much
Thank you very much
You might think it looks hard
All you have to do is start in your backyard.

Sam Davies (9)
Trelewis Primary School, Merthyr Tydfil

Litter

If we recycle we're saving our world
You can make a big difference
Help save our planet!
Don't drop litter
Here's three words to remind you
Reduce, reuse, recycle, yeah
Please recycle and put it in the bin
Recycle paper, plastic bottles too
Just don't forget, one more thing . . .

It's my life, please don't destroy it
Help save our planet, you can do your bit.

Amy Jones (8)
Trelewis Primary School, Merthyr Tydfil

Eco Kids

Don't drop litter on the floor
Tell the people to not drop litter anymore
Respect the environment
Please don't make a dirty dent
We need your help to clean up our act
So join in with us and keep the recycling pact
Don't drop litter on the floor
Otherwise us eco kids will come knocking on your door.

Callum Mayers (9)
Trelewis Primary School, Merthyr Tydfil

Recycle It!

Don't drop litter on the floor
Respect your environment and don't drop any more.

Don't put plastic, paper or tins
Into our rubbish bins.

Reduce
Reuse
Recycle

Recycle it
Recycle it
Recycle *more and more*
Recycle it
Recycle it
And put it by the door!

Caragh Bell-Langford & Kira Thomas (9)
Trelewis Primary School, Merthyr Tydfil

You Can Help

Don't put litter straight in the bin
Recycling is good for almost everything
Do you know where the rubbish goes?
Into the ground in landfills
Right beneath our toes!

Christopher Jones (8) & Morgan Gwilym (9)
Trelewis Primary School, Merthyr Tydfil

Rainforest Poem

R ainforests are in danger
A nimals are losing their homes
I nsects are dying
N early 250,000 rainforest people live there
F lowers are lovely
O r the rosy periwinkle will be extinct
R osy periwinkle is helpful
E very animal will be extinct
S top destroying the rainforest
T he rainforest is a special place for animals to live in.

Callum Crossley (8)
Ysgol Bryn Deva, Connah's Quay

The Rainforest

R ainforests are in danger, please help
A nimals are in danger, please help them live
I t's a fact that the size of a football pitch is destroyed every second
N early all the animals are extinct
F lowers are important, many will soon be gone forever
O xygen is important to us and animals
R osy periwinkles will soon be gone
E very day trees are being cut down
S top the destruction of the rainforest
T he rainforest people will soon have to move home.

Emily Monteith-Roberts (10)
Ysgol Bryn Deva, Connah's Quay

The Rainforest

R ainforests are in trouble
A nimals are in danger
I n danger of extinction
N ever coming back
F orever they will be gone, even the ones that attack
O ver the world the children will weep
R ight down in our hearts, we love the rainforest deeply
E veryone wants it to keep
S ize of a football pitch is gone every second
T he result, one third of the birds live in the rainforest
and soon they will all be gone.

Shannon Baines (9)
Ysgol Bryn Deva, Connah's Quay

The Rainforest

R ainforests are in danger, please help
A nimals live in the rainforest
I t's a fact that half the rainforest has gone
N othing goes to waste on the forest floor
F lowers will soon be gone
O xygen comes from all the trees
R ainforests are found in the tropical parts of the world
E very second the size of a football pitch is destroyed
S top destroying the rainforest now
T rees and plants help cure diseases.

Letitia Lovelock (10)
Ysgol Bryn Deva, Connah's Quay

The Rainforest

There is a problem with logging in the rainforest
They don't know what they're doing
The rainforest is being destroyed
They don't know what homes they're chewing

Do you know how it is destroyed?
It's a technique called slash and burn
We will soon do something about it
We will get our turn.

Daniel Wilson (9)
Ysgol Bryn Deva, Connah's Quay

The Rainforest

R ain is falling in the forest
A nimals running for shelter
I t's an animal going and running
N asty bulldozers coming
F lowers growing and dying
O xygen is getting less every second
R ice is stopping and disaster coming
E very tree has nearly gone
S top killing our forest
T ime to protest now!

Kyle Villiers (10)
Ysgol Bryn Deva, Connah's Quay

The Rainforest

R ainforests are in danger, please help
A nimals are dying
I t's a fact that the rainforest will be destroyed by 2060
N early extinct like the animals that live there
F lowers like the rosy periwinkle cure diseases
O xygen is being lost forever
R ain in the rainforest pours down every night
E very second the size of a football pitch is destroyed
S top the destruction now
T he rate of destruction is not in a good state.

William Williamson (8)
Ysgol Bryn Deva, Connah's Quay

Animal Cruelty

Animal cruelty is a horrible thing
Kicking, hitting and abandoning
The pets all go to the RSPCA
So rescue a pet today
No need to pay, it's all free
So you can make a pet happy
Come down to the RSPCA
And take a pet away.

Kelly Louise Walker (10)
Ysgol Bryn Deva, Connah's Quay

Save Our Animals From Extinction!

'Extinct' means an animal has not been seen in the wild for 50 years
There are many endangered animals in the world which raises
                                  concerns and fears
Pandas, tigers, koalas and great apes are slowly disappearing
                                  from our planet we live on
The growing population and interference with our environment
Means extinction will soon have won
'Why are the animals dying out?' I shout
Stop the pollution, the chopping down of rainforests and every day
                                  new buildings we meet
Because animal habitats are being destroyed
Which means nowhere to live and nothing to eat
What should we do? I urge you . . .
Be green, recycle as much as you can
Protect the planet, you can, you can!
Adopt an animal at your local zoo, this will pay for its keep
                                  and make them happy too
Don't buy products made from animals, like ivory and reptile skin
As now is the time, extinction must end and protecting wildlife
                                              must *begin!*

Alessia Powell (10)
Ysgol Bryn Deva, Connah's Quay

Let's Give More To The Poor

Life is hard for the poor
We should all help to give them more
It's not fair them living on the streets
They need somewhere warm and something nice to eat
The air is bad for them to breathe
The streets they live on are diseased
They wash and drink the dirty water
And still not many people care
We should all lend a hand
Give some money, if only a pound
Every penny goes a long way
To make this world a better place.

Ashleigh Claire Jones (10)
Ysgol Bryn Deva, Connah's Quay

The World Around Us

The world is dying
The air is fading
The people are trying to survive
We recycle and cure
The illness and pollution
But what's going on with the war?
It's peace we all need
The kids are our future
So why don't we pull together a little bit
More!

Philip Goff (10)
Ysgol Bryn Deva, Connah's Quay

Rainforest

R oaring chainsaws
A nimals run
I nto the rainforest
N o one will come
F lowers are dying
O h what a shame
R ainforest crying
E veryone feels its pain
S top killing the rainforest
T hen we will all be happy again.

Deryn Phillips (11)
Ysgol Bryn Deva, Connah's Quay

Rainforest

R ainforests are in danger
A mazon Rainforest is being destroyed
I think I can help, can you?
N early half the birds are in the Amazon Rainforest
F lowers like the periwinkle are important
O h, I don't think it's fair, do you?
R ainforests are at risk
E mergency, you need to help the Amazon Rainforest
S ad animals are losing their homes
T he trees are burnt and the animals are hurt.

Amy Jane Gould (9)
Ysgol Bryn Deva, Connah's Quay

The Rainforest

R ainforests are so beautiful
A nimals that live in the rainforest are becoming extinct
I nsects are all over the place
N early all the rainforests in the world are destroyed
F lowers are important
O ne of the flowers is called the rosy periwinkle
R osy periwinkle is a flower that is used for medicine
E very year 9,000 species are extinct
S ome of the animals have bright patterns on their skin
T he people who destroy the rainforest they are horrible
So stop, stop, *stop!*

Aimee Shaw (10)
Ysgol Bryn Deva, Connah's Quay

Our World

Look out the window
Cars, buses and aeroplanes
What's happening to it?
Forests being cut down
The air turning brown
With all those factories.

We need to save our world
The ice is melting, the Earth dying
Animals losing their lives
We need to save our world.

Tom Blackwell
Ysgol Owen Jones, Northop

Stop! Stop! Stop!

Have you seen the world yet?
Take a peek, it needs a tweak
It used to be a lovely planet
With forests, tourists . . .

Until they came, yes
Those mighty factories
Which kill canaries
Gosh, blimey, stop those gunshots.

Those poor rainforests cut down
Don't just put them down
You clown, look they're not brown
Plant some more and don't chop down.

Everyone help, everybody *stop!*
Or you'll go pop
You don't want that, now give yourself a pat
And stop this now!

Corey Hunt (10)
Ysgol Owen Jones, Northop

Earth

Watching, thinking, as a lorry passes by,
Watching a factory with grey smoke passing by.
Me and my family having a nice day out,
Ruined by litter and big puffs of smoke!

Thinking why this should happen to the world,
A clean healthy planet turned to dirt and to dust.
What did it do? What did it do to you?

Awww look at that hedgehog, it is stuck,
Stuck in an ice cream cone!
There are bins everywhere!
Still no care for the world.

Watching, thinking as a lorry passes by.
Watching a factory with grey smoke passing by.
Me and my family having a nice day out
Ruined by litter and big puffs of smoke!

What did it do? What did it do to you?

Lucie Cansdale
Ysgol Owen Jones, Northop

Our World

Enjoy the world whilst it is green
Stop throwing litter, it is mean
It may seem like a lot of fuss
But factories are choking us
The weather's changing, as you can see
It really is affecting me
The Earth is turning into a mess
It really is in great distress
You might rather use your car
But when you're walking it's not that far
Aeroplanes soaring across the sky
It makes me ask why, oh why?

Chloe Tivendale (11)
Ysgol Owen Jones, Northop

Look Outside

Take a look outside
Open your eyes wide
The global warming's strange
What are we going to change?

I have some concerns
The hot sun burns
The ice caps are melting
The animals need helping
Forests are being cut down
The Earth is making a frown.

We are using too much energy
The world's just like an elegy
Take a look outside
Open your eyes wide!

Cameron Williams (11)
Ysgol Owen Jones, Northop

What's Happened To Our World?

What's happened to the world?
Pollution, global warming and climate change
Beautiful blue skies, now becoming grey
Clouds were white but now are black
Blame the factories and close them
Planes are in the sky all day
Try and keep them far away
What has happened to the world?
Concerned people for the future
What has happened to our nature?
Cars are now rushing up and down
Leaving trails of pollution behind
Use your bicycles and your feet
Please, please help
Do your bit!

Shivani Patel (11)
Ysgol Owen Jones, Northop

The World Change

Me, I like the sea
I also like climbing a tree
All of this will go to waste
If we don't stop global warming at a pace.

Have you looked out the window lately?
It's winter and the sun is bright
And the snow isn't there at night.

Me, I like the sea
Between you and me
I'll miss being in a tree.

Katie Gemmell (11)
Ysgol Owen Jones, Northop

Our Wonderful World

Thoughtless thieves dropping litter
Opening our atmosphere
Stitch the wound and walk not drive
Take the pavement not a drive.

We want to live
But we need something to live in
We can't live in a broken world
So help our home like we help each other.

Don't be a thoughtless thief
And put your litter in the bin.

Nicole Askey (11)
Ysgol Owen Jones, Northop

Thoughtless, Mindless People

Thoughtless, mindless people of our world
No idea of what they are doing
When will it end?
When will it stop?
The unfairness
Why do people have to be so careless?

Do not complain
About the rain
It's our fault
Pollution, factories, planes and cars
It's our fault about the rain
So you can't go and complain!

Litter, paper, cans of Coke
The binmen's trucks creating smoke
Help take the gas-guzzling monsters off the road
Do your bit
Recycling should do it!

Jack Hewitt (10)
Ysgol Owen Jones, Northop

Look After Earth

L ook outside, and what can you see?
O h, how beautiful the world is
O nly we can keep it that way
K angaroos, elephants, should be here forever.

A ll of us are ruining our world
F orgetting to put our rubbish in the bin
T oo many factories causing pollution
E veryone can help the world
R eady to change, because I am

E veryone can help our home
A nd then we can live our lives with no worrying
R easons to change the world could go on forever
T he world is our home, don't ruin it
H elp us, please!

Olivia Farrell
Ysgol Owen Jones, Northop

Think

L ook out of the window
O ur world decreasing rapidly
O ur world dying from over-fuelling
K eep checking out the window

A fter a short while, you, me, no more
F orever changing
T he beautiful air, smell
E verlasting beauty could die
R apidly dying

O ur environment
U se your brain
R ethink

W atch out
O ur world is going, going
R each for the bin
L ook, listen, beware
D o you think the world will last? You decide.

Conal Ghee
Ysgol Owen Jones, Northop

Have You Looked Outside?

Have you looked outside
To see the planet falling?
If you listen carefully, you'll hear the planet calling
Will you help? Will you help? Will you do your bit?
And help our planet live
To keep Mother Nature
And save nature
For all of you
How would you feel if you were falling?
Scared, upset, down?
Have you looked outside
To see the planet falling?
If you listen carefully, you'll hear the planet calling.

Tanya Van Ruth
Ysgol Owen Jones, Northop

Young Writers Information

We hope you have enjoyed reading this book - and that you will continue to enjoy it in the coming years.

If you like reading and writing poetry drop us a line, or give us a call, and we'll send you a free information pack.

Alternatively if you would like to order further copies of this book or any of our other titles, then please give us a call or log onto our website at www.youngwriters.co.uk

**Young Writers Information
Remus House
Coltsfoot Drive
Peterborough
PE2 9JX
(01733) 890066**